I0841139

PATTERNS & DESIGNS

Adult Coloring Book

50 Creations For Active Mind & Healthy Brain

SevenFairiesColoring.Com

ISBN: 9781726754903

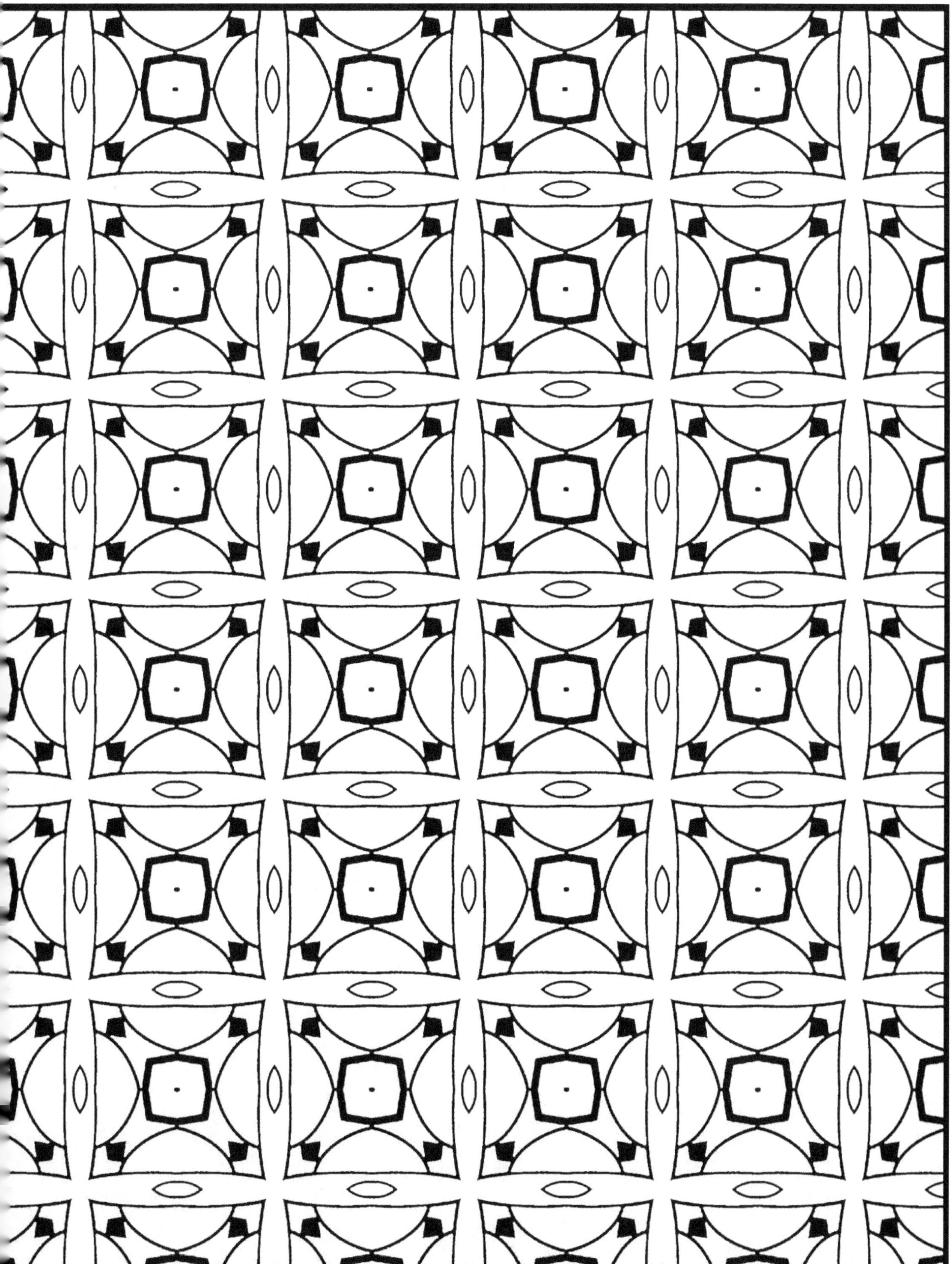

Thank you.

www.ingramcontent.com/pod-product-compliance
Lightning Source LLC
Chambersburg PA
CBHW081952260726
48657CB00009BA/2682